Before the Big Bang Makes a Sound

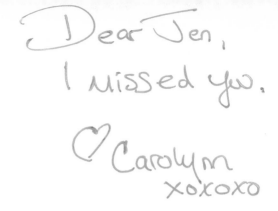

Dear Jen,
I missed you.
♡ Carolynn
xoxoxo

Before the Big Bang Makes a Sound

Poems by

Carolynn Kingyens

Cover design by Shay Culligan

ISBN: 978-1-950462-69-8

Kelsay Books Inc.

kelsaybooks.com

502 S 1040 E, A119
American Fork, Utah 84003

For Rob, Esme, and Eloise

"Oh," she says, "you're changing."
But we're always changing.

Counting Crows, "Anna Begins"
August and Everything After

Acknowledgments

Across the Margin: "Abundant Life," "Small as a Mouse," "Break the Mirror in Your Youth," "Coney Island"

Boxcar Literary Journal: "After the Reception"

Eunoia Review: "The Attic" "The Northerners"

Glass; Journal of Poetry: "Remains of a Crime Scene"

Nthanda Review: "Autoimmune" "Broken Boxcars," "Fantasy Meeting"

Silenced Press: "Silent Treatment," previous title, "Washing Dishes"

The Potomac: "The Weight of Words"

Red Eft Review: "Bathroom Crucifix," "Desperado," "No One is Immune," "85th & West End," previous title, "Fate"

Tuck Magazine, Human Rights & Arts: "High Anxiety," "The Abyss," "Of Mice, Of Men, Of Chickens," "Freakish Accidents," "High Anxiety," "You Can't Handle the Truth," "Last Summer"

Contents

Autoimmune

Some diseases take time
to manifest,
turning your body
against your body slowly;
cellular changes so subtle
they are imperceptible
for decades;
through the birth
of your daughter,
death of your mother,
through the drawn-out
divorce from Richard-Dick,
never truly believing him
when he said he loved you;
through the five-day,
cross-country move
when you turned forty;
buying a two-bedroom
bungalow in Venice Beach,
painting the house colors
you wouldn't normally
choose—lime-green,
salmon-pink,
banana-yellow, ocean-blue.

You adopt a stray cat
you name Kerouac.
He trusts you over time,
brushing his lean,
black body against your
ankles every morning,
purring, both of you
content.

It starts with numbness,
that pins-and-needles
feeling, the way your limbs
suddenly fall flat-asleep
when sitting cross-legged
for too long.

Next the twitching
and random falling
that embarrass you at first—
before the diagnosis,
before you learn
your disease could
be named.

Of Mice, of Men, of Chickens

I come from a long line
of women who can break
a man's heart
and a chicken's neck.

Their gingham aprons
full of white feathers;
small hands
full of beating hearts.

Bowls of blood
sausage and stale bread
for days.

Of mice and men;
of men and mice,
of chickens,
it doesn't matter.

And my father,
a projection of defeat
inside the house he built
with his own hands.

Somewhere along the line,
I jumped the continuum.

Not all invasions
are Trojan.
Some are innocuous
as a slip of skin
at the right time.

Coney Island

Tonight, I will blame
the oysters, and then again,
I always have the rain.

It's raining cats and dogs.
It's raining bullets.
It's raining men—
Hallelujah, Amen!

I want to go back in time
where hope hangs heavier
than the moon;
when love is hard as a fist
inside the throat;
a time when real butterflies
replace the redundancy
of roller coasters.

Once I read a Heraclitus
quote spray painted
on the side
of a Bronx bodega:

No man ever steps
in the same river twice,
for it's not the same river
and he's not the same man.

I drive to Coney Island
to smell the piss and pot,
on the way to forgetting
your name.

Bathroom Crucifix

The first time I touched
a crucifix
I was five years old
in my grandmother's
powder-blue bathroom,
unaware of suffering
and sacrifice;
unaware of the million
and one ways
a sinner could torture
a saint and still get away
with it, when I felt
compelled to caress
Christ's hard, flexed veins
arched away
from his shin bones,
muscles, pretty feet.

The crucifix was nailed
to the floral pattern wall
above the light switch—
Christ's eyes forever
cast down
staring at my grandmother's
personal things;
her nighttime rituals—
boxes of Polident
rosary beads
little jars of beauty cream
and an old photo
of her only son
my father, forever a boy
dressed for Holy

Communion, mimicking
the face of innocence;
wedged securely
inside the edge
of the switch.

After the Reception

You check out Simone
Oliver as she snakes
by us in a fitted, black
sheath dress that shows
off her arms, well-toned
from carrying her twins
from Beijing.

Tonight, she was suddenly
sexy in the afterglow
of conversation
as I shape-shifted
into something
inanimate and dense—
a floor lamp turned off,
a hard-back chair
unoccupied,
a mantel balancing a clock,
candles, car keys of guests.

I am your homely wife,
whom you will later
undress and devour
after the reception,
in the bed-cover darkness.

The Attic

It's years later when you
find yourself back here
kneeling on the barnacle
board, attic floor
looking for the glass-spun
ornaments wrapped
delicately in yellow-tinged
paper, and those precious
decorations made by the
small hands of your small
children, who are now
grown and distant,
when you spot that
dust-laden time capsule
buried behind boxes
of old baby clothes
and tax filings.

You drag the capsule
into the middle of the attic
where you sit and straddle
your past like an open gift—
thumbing through pictures
of your pre-baby body,
smoking a cigarette
in a white bikini
leaning back on a wooden
railing somewhere in the
middle of hot Texas.

You stare into those
squinty eyes of that happy
and still hopeful girl,
who is unaware
of all the kneeling to come.

You Can't Handle the Truth

Tell me the truth,
and I will follow you
through wormwood,
wormholes, to the place
where the worm
never dies.

I've looked for Christ
inside the echoes
of St. John the Divine;
inside cerebral chat rooms,
and their theological
debates; in the downcast
eyes of the homeless.

Salvatore—salutation—
salvation.

I used to believe salvation
was simple until I read
the demons believe
and tremble.

What does it mean
to work out your salvation
with fear and trembling?

The senses lie by omission;
ask any pilot who has
pulled the plane out
of a graveyard spiral—
spatial disorientation.

The ego, the door
I stubbed my big toe on.

Yet I am to trust
I've been born of water
and the Spirit?

Christ says His sheep
will hear His voice;
I am listening.

Freakish Accidents

After my move
to Manhattan,
a gust of wind blew down
a 4-by-8 sheet of plywood
from atop a condo
conversion in the West
Village, striking a woman
in the head—killing her
instantly as she walked
on the sidewalk below,
at the clearing
of scaffolding.

In overcast Ithaca,
I'd watched a wind storm,
from the safety
of my living room,
blow down a grand
ash tree; my pitched roof
breaking its fall.

When the winds picked up,
I moved my daughters,
still sleeping, to the middle
of my bed.

The pine trees on Pine Tree
Road swayed in the black
hole wind at night,
their haunting sound
reminiscent
of ceremonious gongs.

Each gong for a loss.
Each gong for a betrayal.

The Abyss

Once on the A Train
an old woman
with milky eyes
stared at me for too long;
and I remembered
Nietzsche's warning:

*And when you gaze long
into an abyss, the abyss
gazes also into you.*

So I said an inward prayer,
and did not look back
when I got off at West 4th St.

In New York,
we have salves, oils,
candles and trinkets—
a cure-all for bad vibes,
the evil eye,
generational curses.

In the Bronx—
La Santa Muerte.

Today, I will meditate
on Muhammad—
the kind bodega owner
who calls Lucy,
his sweet tabby,
up from the dark cellar,
where she's been sleeping
or killing,

so my daughters
can pet her;
so my daughters
can smile.

Tomorrow, I will open
my eyes in anticipation
of a new morning.

I will turn and marvel
at your eclipsed soul-body
still sleeping.

Break the Mirror in Your Youth

I used to go without a bra
once, too; breasts—smooth
and shiny as two eggplants
under a tank top,
under the umbrella—
all the boys' stares, heavy
as breath on my back.

The beauty of babes
is currency.

But beauty has less
of a shelf life
than vegetable oil
and MSG.

Tony Tucci once confessed
he takes all his first dates
out for Chinese food:

You know, he said,
those shitty ones
with the fluorescent lights;
real, unattractive lighting.

If she still looks hot
under them lights,
then I know she's a keeper.

Fluorescent lights don't lie
like we do.

Today, a stale cookie
shaped like a deformed
pilgrim collar tells me:

Break the mirror
in your youth.

Abundant Life

In time, all the bananas
will go black in the cracked,
cerulean bowl—
a Brooklyn treasure
found on a stranger's stoop.

Here, front stoop
means free stuff.
Here, fruit is an hourglass.
Here, Seal is Morpheus.

We're never going to
survive/unless we get a
*little crazy/*his song goes.

And I am crazy about squid
and shitake, sinew and
cartilage; not caring
what I look like, sucking
the fish bone-broth dry
like a savage,
double-fisting the pretty,
embroidered bowl.

We keep making the same
sake toast, until you do
your drunk De Niro,
and I begin
to see you in a new light.

We walk the extra blocks
to listen to the bells
of St. Agnes a little more.

And I think *This must be*
the abundant life, when
Christ's cup overflows.

Small as a Mouse

I mistook tolerance as love
for so long, I grew small
and quiet, a mouse
making a home
inside a load-bearing wall,
content with a matchstick
bed and wedge of Swiss.

My high frequency
heartbeat tortured the cat,
but no one else
in that house.

Even now, I still apologize—
Sorry, you bumped into me;
Sorry, you got even
over a perceived slight;
Sorry, for your spreading
lies so convincingly,
I lost my past
and present at once.

My friend, by contrast,
grew stoic and unmovable.

The last time we met
for drinks at the pub,
we were two shadows lost
in conversation—
one big as a brownstone,
the other small as a mouse.

The Weight of Words

Some words bear enough
weight to incite mass mobs
in closed spaces,
words like *FIRE!*
words like *He has a Gun!*
Imagine the people's panic:
their pushing and pulling
down, crawling
to the nearest exits for life.

Now imagine a naive girl
who hasn't learned respect
for the weighty-word
never, who uses it
too loosely when speaking
like *I'll never do that*
to only do precisely *that*
and more.

After making anniversary
love, he takes a shower
as I flip through
the channels
in search of a talk show.

Silent Treatment

He watched her walk away
from another fight,
watched her turn from him
to embrace the afternoon
shining through
an open window,
above the kitchen sink
where she watched
their boys from a distance
chase the neighbor's calico
up a Japanese maple
where it panted for life
on a limb too high
for their small,
outstretched hands.

She turned her attention
back to washing dishes,
and washed so rigorously,
the teacups clapped
their saucers,
spoons, oval moons,
eclipsed rims of coffee
mugs, butter knives slid
inside the fork in forks.

And it was a surprise
when he walked up
behind her to rub the nape
of her neck, gently gliding
his hand down the length

of her arm, into the warm,
sudsy water, where he
found her hands hiding
under the shelter
of a capsized bowl.

Broken Boxcars

Comfort is cruel as fruit
tucked inside the warmth
of wicker, left alone
to the inevitable—
the bruise-brown rot
dimpling the skin
when touched, or the
subject of a novice
painter's whimsical
translation; either way—
doomed.

Lennon knew about the
addiction to creature
comforts, how it keeps us
away from our best selves
when he said:

*Life is what happens to you
while you're busy making
other plans.*

I imagine my father
was once busy
making plans, too.
Now he is the perfect
example of the potato—
preferring the confines
of a couch over the choices
of a hot drifter, whom I
once invited home to dinner.

Everything the
earth-smelling,
dreadlocked nomad
owned could fit inside
his backpack.

The rest, he said,
is immaterial; the rest,
he said, *is dullness;*
and dullness, he said,
is a switchblade held
to the throat during
a soul-jack.

The drifter's absolute
freedom irked my father,
who was forever bound
to his loyalties—
an aloof, dying mother
a hoarder ex-wife
a refi-mortgage, and me—
a lone wolf line of broken
boxcars he could never
escape from, at least
in good conscience.

Remains of a Crime Scene

Black birds pumped
their puppet-like wings
for distance, for air-cover
coasting into narrow-arrow
darts, into sharp
exclamation points;
these synchronized,
feathered air-swimmers
with their manipulated
aerodynamic cartilage—
flat as dinner plates,
circling the flesh,
the bones, the wreckage
through the fissures,
the fractures
through the gaps
in the texture of trees;
hearty foliage sheltering
this sin, before the black
bears arrived,
before the black
birds began their circling.

Fantasy Meeting

Let's say we run into
one another unplanned,
at Grand Central Station
at rush hour;
marching among the mobs,
those coming and going,
dragging their wheeled-
weight luggage through
the marble station
to the stereo-sounds
of routine announcements
by a man with a thick
New York accent,
who is standing behind
official-looking plexiglass,
announcing delays
and early arrivals,
a lost child, or found tickets.

It's here, among the chaos,
where we will meet.
I'm hot again in this
fantasy meeting—
successful, a card-carrying
somebody, someone you
would never expect I'd
turn out to be,
and your eyes will tell
of your regret.

We'll exchange superficial
greetings as strangers
often do, and lie about
pending plans and exciting
lives back home.

You will try to forget
the Florida-shaped birthmark
on my thigh, and I will try
to forget the surgical scar
on your shoulder blade
from a ski accident
in Aspen when you
were twelve, kissing it
that night I saw you naked
and vulnerable
inside my doorway.

The Northerners

It seemed we moved
into new houses
every two years;
getting up early
those first mornings
with loud yawns,
an exaggerated stretch,
almost contentment.

Even our neighbors
were shiny and new—
at first; and at first,
we were open,
taking them up on their
generous invitations
of summer-fun BBQs,
and southern fish fries;
you in the center of hunters,
fishermen, men who liked
to work with their hands—
a man's man: the kind
my father respected,
and took at their word.

How uncomfortable
you looked standing there,
holding a cold Sam Adams,
bobbing your head
in agreement
on the art of deer hunting,
aware your dear wife
loved animals;

how I covered my eyes
as we drove by
their broken,
awkwardly-bent carcasses
strewn on the side of roads.

You watched me
from across the deck, too,
sitting at a picnic table
with their chatty wives,
dressed in black-knit jersey,
wearing my beloved,
amber-colored beads.

You noticed the nuance
in our styles—
the women in their pink
and butter-yellow Polo's,
their white-shroud Capri's,
how their clothes
reflected the afternoon sun
instead of absorbing it.

You couldn't understand
why every sentence
started and ended with *Honey*
like *Honey, I'll get that,* or
You don't want to do that, Honey.

It was a little too intimate
for Northerners.

No One is Immune

Baby, don't you wanna dance up on me?
—Britney Spears

A pillowcase stuff full
of cold cash is dumped
over the head
of a buxom blonde
naked atop an unmade
bed in a hot mess motel
the color of puke
somewhere south
of Rio Grande.

Later, in a convertible
he carjacked, she'll take
the wheel—and do donuts
where a lake used to be,
stirring a dust-bowl the size
of Dallas as he fires off
his gun into the air
for no other reason
than crazy.

Their door mat reads:
*My Consequences Don't
Live Here Anymore,*
and for a while, this is true.

But a house built on shot
glasses, pill bottles
and ash trays will age
a body strangely—
broken biology,
Freakonomics,
the way a fresh face

can turn into a catch-all
mitt, weathered before
its time; the way a delicate
voice can turn into the bark
of a seal, while the body,
from the neck down,
remains preserved
much longer.

The buxom blonde will rock
those daisy dukes, tank tops,
and cowboy boots
just like her favorite, aging
pop-princess, who shakes
her money-maker
night after night
on the Vegas Strip,
singing the same old songs;
dancing the same old
hip-hop moves
she did when she was 18
as her fans, who have aged
along with her,
scream her name in ecstasy
in the encore.

No one sees those swollen
joints she ices after each
show, cursing the
crookedness
that is her industry.

But the body, like time,
continues to keep score
on all of us, and no one
is immune.

West 85th & West End

Every day a new page turns
above the beanstalk;
above the disco-ball-moon
and fog-machine clouds,
where an unamused angel
finger-flicks an arrow
affixed to a wheel,
spinning indefinitely,
an eternity.

Down here, I knock
on my neighbor's door
in search of time—
not egg, flour, or a cup
of hourglass sugar
for my invisible cake.

It's no coincidence
we dash to markets,
clearing shelves
of bread first—
hunker down
when the storm comes;
when the storm
is christened a name—
Lilly, Olive, Coltrane—
the name of my daughter's
first grade friend,
whose father works
at the U.N.;
trilingual, plays chess
like an old man.

Trouble is a loose brick,
fifteen floors up, at the co-op
on West 85th & West End,
where an inviting bench awaits
impending doom.

Last Summer

We buried the baby bunny
in a Brooks Brothers box
under the moss tree
in the corner of our yard.

It was our eagle-eyed
daughter who spotted it
from the back door;
thinking, at first, it was
a wad of hair, and then,
a fallen bird's nest.

You skimmed the dead
baby bunny out of the
pool for us; laying it
before bare feet in our
circle of curiosity.

The girls insisted on a
proper burial so your
mother, a retired florist,
made up two small
bouquets from the garden—
black-eyed Susan, morning
glory, a few white
hydrangeas, tying it together
with twine she found
from the shed—a bouquet
for each granddaughter
to lay atop the bunny's
grave.

Your father said a quiet
prayer, and I recited a poem
that never became a poem:

God's breath is inside you,
and so the bunny.

High Anxiety

Squint into the white
horizon just over the sand
dunes, down the street
from the dive bar,
an F-bomb away
from spontaneous
combustion—exploding
particles—gun smoke,
a sneeze, the way a shaft
of light illuminates
the dust mite; static energy,
neediness, sleep paralysis;
the jump-scares
from dollar store, bake pans
springing inside preheated
ovens; a heart grown tired
of its chronic techno
house beat; the pet bird
made bald from missing
its master; movie trailers,
sleep-eating, raw-juicing;
the incessant meows
of a deaf cat;
fingers gesture a flesh-gun
now pointing to the head,
a thumb hovers
over an invisible trigger,
before the big bang
makes a sound.

Desperado

Two women, no relation,
both exited a Whole Foods
in somewhat succession,
walked past my Audi Q5,
idling in front.

The first woman wore
jeans, the color of a sand
dollar, and a lemon
meringue-colored sweater
that highlighted her dewy
skin as she sashayed.

'Yale Law' emblazoned
in bold text on both sides
of her canvas bag,
in case I missed it,
filled, I imagined,
with delicacies
for a backyard boil—
corn on the cob,
red bliss potatoes;
shrimp—crawfish—
sausage; a bottle
of chilled Riesling.

A man, around the same
age as my father, also sat
idling across from me
inside his Silverado
when the sashayed-one,
a perfect vision,
walked between the chasm

our cars made in the
Whole Foods' parking lot.

I watched him, watching
her as she walked toward
her Range Rover.

The second woman,
in contrast, wore black
yoga pants stained with
bronze streaks I recognized
from a mist of spray-bleach.

Hair, hurried-damp;
facial features, much fuller,
as she appeared to carry the
burdens of the world
inside her brown paper bag.

The older man kept
inching his Silverado
into the woman's path,
his face showing
annoyance.

I have seen that look
before on my father's face
the time he asked me
to skim the aftermath
of a summer storm
from atop the surface
of the pool.

And when my skim-job
didn't meet the standard,
he would snatch the gigantic
butterfly net out
of my hand, turn his
whole body away from me,
and shake his big, square head—
a head, I thought,
looked like the shape
of a thumb.

The Parable of Time

In New York, the city that
never sleeps, Time is boss.
She owns us, but we still
rush to beat the clock;
rush to beat rush hour—
strangers in a sea
of strangers bum-rushing
subway doors like cattle.
Time laughs.
Time taps her long fingers
on the table, and somewhere
in the Bronx a leaky faucet
drips to the rhythm
of her tapping.

Time has many daughters—
Deja Vu (Deja),
Irony,
History,
Regret,
and the toughest
of them all - Karma.
They are her agents,
her reapers.

And to the maniacal ones
in power, who have long
forgotten Time and her
daughters, Time says,
"Give it some time."

Time is boss.
Time will tell like a snitch.
She will sing like a canary.

Never Look Back

Oh, the drudgery
of nostalgia,
the sentimental—
strange hoarders of ghosts.

About the Author

Carolynn Kingyens was born and raised in Northeast Philadelphia. She grew up in a row home, the youngest of seven children.

Her poems have been featured in *Boxcar Poetry Journal, The Potomac, Glass: Journal of Poetry, The Orange Room Review, Red Eft Review, Across the Margin, Eunoia Review, Tuck Magazine, Schuylkill Valley Journal, Haggard & Halloo, Word Riot,* and *Nthanda Review*. She was nominated for Best New Poets by *Silenced Press*.

Carolynn often draws inspiration from the Earnest Hemmingway quote: *All you have to do is write one true sentence. Write the truest sentence that you know.*

Today, Carolynn lives in New York City with her husband, and their two kind, funny, and creative daughters.

Made in the USA
Middletown, DE
21 January 2020